LET

THERE

BE

BUSINESS

SPEAKING YOUR BUSINESS INTO EXISTENCE
Featuring 7 Methods of Preparation

TEIA ACKER, MBA, BS

FOREWORD BY
MOSES CALHOUN, III

LET
THERE
BE
BUSINESS

Teia A. Acker, MBA

Let There Be Business

ISBN-13:978-1973718383
ISBN-10:1973718383

© Copyright 2017 Teia Alicia Acker

Ebony & Ivory Professional Services

All photos / Illustrations by Teia Alicia Acker © 2013

Front & Back Cover designed by EIPS, INC of Atlanta, Georgia.

Edited by Tyrone Avery Acker for T. A. Acker, LLC.

This book is dedicated to every individual aspiring to become successful in launching a business. You can do this......Simply close your eyes and say:

"LET THERE BE......BUSINESS"

To Kenneth Brown,

Thank you for lighting the fire to my life.
It is because of you I am reminded that
"success comes to those who create it."

To Judy Whilhite- Mincey,

*Thank you for teaching and enforcing the gift
of reading. Twenty-eight years later and it
still one of my greatest accomplishments.*

———————————

*To the world's best group of friends,
behind every great woman, is a group of ladies
cheering her on in a group text. Thank you for being
my biggest support system.*

———————————

*To my greatest assets, Trey & Trinity...
Thank you is an understatement. I love You both!*

———————————

Mom & Dad...... Thank You!

"Your purpose is to make your audience see what you saw, hear what you heard, feel what you felt. Relevant detail, couched in concrete, colorful language, is the best way to recreate the incident as it happened and to picture it for the audience."

-Dale Carnegie

LET THERE BE BUSINESS...

| Table of Contents |

| Foreword |

By Moses Calhoun, III

Teia Acker is a woman I am proud to call my friend, but most importantly, my business colleague. It isn't the fact that she has successfully completed over 500 resumes and cover letters, though that is extremely impressive. It isn't her constant words of encouragement and motivation for which she provides daily to her fellow constituents. It isn't the fact that she endlessly seeks ways to help others, whether it is in business or personal. It is simply because she believes in helping others "GET NOTICED".

Teia Acker has collaborated with me on many large projects over the past few years. Our connection is one of valued respect and we share common goals in our desire to provide quality services. Although she always said she has learned much from me, I must say that I have learned as much or more from her. While I have instilled in her a "never say I don't do" attitude, she has taught me the value of having a team of professionals working with me, because no one can do it all alone.

Teia is hardworking. She is focused, committed, professional, tenacious, compassionate, a go getter, and a true believer in what she pursues. When we collaborate on projects, I can depend on her to do 150% of her part!

Since we have met, I have been following her growth. Her passion for what she does is unmatched; from offering resume services at a reduced rate for persons who were suddenly laid off, to helping non-profit organizations obtain 501(c)3 status, Teia goes all out to help her clients.

I can say that Teia Acker is a rising star, an international talent, and a wonderful colleague who I am looking forward to working with on future bigger and better projects. Her words command attention. As Teia discusses in this book, there is significance in understanding how to speak dreams into reality. While relating it to the beginning facets of business, Teia introduces the importance of maintaining balance, a mental as well as physical checklist, a willingness to understand what is important in business as well as how to ensure sustainability in business.

I challenge anyone who has ever desired to have a business and are simply unsure of what to do, where to go, how to begin or who to call, to simply read Teia's message and gain the understanding of a lifetime. Her words make the most difficult aspects of business seem so simple. As an established business owner, there are several areas of this book that enabled me to re-examine my practices. As if the #7 was not significant enough, Teia managed to capture my attention as to how I can continue my business in the future. Her words offer more than a "how –to" manual could ever bring. Her words speak hope. Let There Be....

| Preface |

"If people like you, they'll listen to you, but if they trust you, they'll do business with you"

-Zig Ziglar

After taking the time to invest in my business and its upcoming fourth year, I reflected on the components of business they gave me the greatest struggle. I begin to think about all of the aspects of business that most people miss out on because they are so anxious and so ready to begin. They are also so adamant to have a business that they forget how important it is to have things polished before getting started. It is also important to remember that nothing, not even the world, was created without a thought.

Upon deciding to entitle this book "Let There Be", I recanted on the days when I had to encourage myself, speak positivity within myself and rely on the word of God. I begin to find strength through the believe of those things that I desire to become.

There were times when it did not seem as though the business was going to flourish in the way I had hoped or dreamed it to be. In fact, many times there did not seem to be enough evidence of the business or that I was chosen by God to bring it to pass. There were times I thought God had forgotten about me. There were times I question every moment I spent inside of a classroom, every moment I sat inside a church and every moment I spent holding a meaningful conversation with someone I consider to be wise. Eventually, I was reminded that everything that I needed was in the word of God and essentially the one thing that I needed was in his book.

I searched and I searched. I went from chapter to chapter while studying characters such as Ruth and Naomi. I also studied Eve, Mary and Martha. Essentially, I characterize my life on the premise of the proverbs 31 woman. Unknowingly, I found myself trying to depict and transform myself into these women in hopes of capturing the true meaning of becoming a successful woman and most importantly a successful business woman.

When the women of the Bible did not grab my full attention, I then turn to who I considered to be successful women in general. I started following women like Oprah Winfrey, Beyoncé Carter, Condoleezza Rice, and Michelle Obama (to name a few). I navigated through books and magazines about growing companies and success. I began to reflect daily on the words of John Maxwell, Les Brown, and Jim Rohn. Lastly, I began following an outlet for which many businesswomen and men utilize to help launch their dreams of becoming an entrepreneur: the world of social media.

I started following people who I believe had reached the pinnacle of success, as well as those who look the part of success. I began to question myself, stating "if these people are successful and we're serving the same God, why have I not become successful"? I became intrigued by the notion that I had not reached the pinnacle of success but I had acquired education, training and leadership skills.

The feeling of having acquired so much in such a short period of time (while still pondering over what was to come) was beginning to defeat me. I began to feel sorry for myself. I remember sitting on my sofa thinking about getting a divorce after eight years of marriage, facing eviction on a home I had rented (with intentions to purchase through a lease-to-buy program), holding an electricity bill that was past due, and not knowing how I was going to care for the two children God had placed in my life. I felt empty and was unsure if I could return to the workforce that had previously laid me off three times from my position.

While in that space, God whispered in my ears: "Teia, what's in your hands? I need you to utilize the gift that is in your hands." After hearing God speak directly to me, I decided to do exactly what He had informed. I decided to start my own business. I knew that I wanted to help other people become successful. I spoke to my business in the same tone and same voice in which He had spoken on the first day he created the earth. God said: "*Let there be light*" (Genesis1:3) and there was light. I decided to and say "let there be business" and hence, we are here today.

LET

THERE

BE

BUSINESS

| Introduction |

*"And God said, "Let there be light,"
and there was light". Genesis 1:3 NIV*

When God spoke to the heavens and said "Let there be light and there was light, he was essentially speaking to a void in the Earth. He was addressing the need for something to exist that had not. Being the same God who created everything by speaking it into existence revealed metaphorically that we, his children, have the power to speak light into our situations and circumstances. Thusly, to include speaking prosperity and growth into our businesses, the power to become successful in business derives from one's ability to speak it into existence. This type of power is expressed through faith and the belief that we are only limited by the boundaries we set.

When entering the realm of business, there are essentially seven methods encompassed in the notion of speaking business into existence. Seven is the number of competition in the spiritual sense. It signifies the completion of God's work. As a follower of this practice many will be able to complete the business God placed in their paths of purpose.

It is important to remember that business growth and prosperity dwells in the power of the tongue. I task readers to ask God to bless their hands as they seek their purpose and grow their businesses. Afterwards, open those eyes get off those knees, open those mouths and say **"LET THERE BE....... BUSINESS".**

| 1 |

Let There BE "An Idea"
Making It All Make Sense

"*Everything begins with an idea*"
~ *Earl Nightingale*

Let There Be Business

If you look at any business, it is easy to see the success, the accomplishments, the financial status, the popularity, and so on. There are several aspects to business—the planning, the marketing, and more (to be discussed later), but none more important than the idea that starts it all. The idea stems from what my brother and I call the three Ps: *problems, passions, and people.* Collectively, these three attributes serve a *purpose.* It is the name of a business that gives it an identity, but the ideas and thoughts feed its purpose.

An effective business can come from situations where there is a crisis. The need to resolve a *problem,* will spark an idea by an entrepreneur—one that either never existed or has existed but did not work effectively. Many non-profit and for-profit organizations seek solutions to something in the world around them.

Some successful businesses derive from a love for something—service, people, or an activity (such as sports). The *passion* for that one thing is what drives entrepreneurs to wake up every day ready to build, grow, and/or improve something. They see an avenue for their passions or create one.

Lastly, great ideas must serve someone in some capacity. Therefore, *people* are part of any great idea. Sneaker companies must think about the athlete's needs and wants. Beauty product companies must relate to customers who buy their gels, sprays, and more. After all,

Let There Be "An Idea"

if the people aren't supporting you, you have no business. (We will talk more about *people* when we discuss marketing.)

Brainstorming

No idea is perfect. Still, what makes an idea worth pursuing is the process of brainstorming that one puts into it. When a person sits down and brainstorms, he or she is setting boundaries so the idea has distinction and isn't too broad. Brainstorming is setting up charts to compare pros and cons, or strengths and weaknesses. There is more than one way to brainstorm. Brainstorming promotes great planning and can prevent a business from falling into financial, social, and/or physical traps in the future.

There is another 'p' word that I did not mention, and that is *profit*. I understand that anyone who owns a business hopes to earn a profit. There is nothing wrong with that being a goal. But, have an idea that makes an impact beyond a dollar amount. Make consumers feel like they are important to you and not just their money.

| 2 |

Let There BE "Training & Education"
Seeking Counsel Prior To Beginning Business

"Education is that whole system of human training within and without the school house walls, which molds and develops men"

-W.E.B. Du Bois

Let There Be Business

A person can have a great business idea, feel confident, and optimistic about success. Yet, the business may not flourish as planned if that aspiring individual fails to recognize areas of inexperience and seek ways to learn or improve them. Having a strong business may require you to learn several aspects of it—logistics, finances, legal structure, marketing, and so on. Education and/or training should be appropriate to the needs of the business, and at the same time, remain cost-effective. Advancement among members *of* the business can spark increased growth *for* the business.

Formal education vs. Informal education

If we were to look at familiar businesses around us, some owners have college degrees in their respective fields, and possibly years of expertise in other business arenas in lesser roles. They have worked and studied the business model, earned promotions to higher positions (which gave them more insight to the business model), and eventually ventured out on their own to begin their personal business dream. However, there are those entrepreneurs that do not have college degrees, but still have the necessary attributes to run a successful business. They, too, may have had background experiences in a similar business and used their experience, inquiry, courage, and drive to launch themselves into their own arena. So which method is the correct one for you?

Let There Be "Training & Education"

When wanting to start a business, consider both formal and informal education methods. For example, let's say that you are a self-taught piano player. You only know how to play by ear. Can you be successful as a musician and make money playing in your style? Yes, you can. Now, think about what may happen if you took classes on how to read and write notes, rests, and time signatures on music scores. Think about what you could learn from joining an association or club that not only performs but educates members on marketing one's talent. Education can open doors to new connections and opportunities and believe it or not, there is always more to learn about any profession or career choice.

Aspiring entrepreneurs should seek ways to blend their skills and talents with business structure familiarity. Often, we think that talent and drive are enough, but then lack understanding of business in areas such as accounting, legal structure, taxation, and marketing. Do not get me wrong—drive, character, attitude, and talent can take people very far in their pursuit for success. Not every field is the same, and neither is the educational background behind it. Adequate research of similar business models can provide information about what degrees, certifications, or licenses are required to maintain an active status of that business.

At what cost?

We all know that college education carries a price tag. Aspiring entrepreneurs should not carry the emotional burden of trying to pursue a degree that is too expensive. For example, an engineer who makes a very good living, has a talent for creating art. If he is making sufficient money drawing and painting portraits on the side, pursuing a degree in Art or Art History is only beneficial if the "side business" can afford the tuition and fees, books, and other supplies. Otherwise, personal finances can take the hit of college costs, with no guarantee that an increase in business revenue will occur. As an alternative, maybe taking a class on how to expand your business, or how to market art and artists can be more beneficial to where that artist is currently.

Again, if you obtain scholarships or grants to pursue higher education, and you know that learning more aspects of a certain field can only make your business more profitable, then you should consider formal education. A major in Art, coupled with a minor in Business Management or Education may give more options if the engineer's artwork is not selling at a consistent pace. Sometimes, continuing education can benefit one's business in the form to workshops, seminars or classes that aren't as strenuous as the pursuit of a college degree (be it 2 or 4 years). These smaller settings can still provide valuable information and may not cost as much. Besides, one may not need education on the skill itself and could devote more time, energy, and resources toward another important aspect— branding.

| 3 |

Let There BE "A Brand"
Securing the Identity of Your Business

"Your brand is the single most investment you can make in your business"
-Steve Forbes

Let There Be Business

With many business ideas, originality does not just exist in the idea itself, but rather, in how that idea is presented. You may have an idea to open a coffee shop, knowing that many coffee shops already exist. You may want to start a clothing line, knowing that several exist in one store alone. To separate your business from other similar businesses, you must focus on *branding*. Branding essentially gives a business its visual, mental, and emotional identity.

If we are honest with ourselves, we value outward appearance. We want others to look at who we are and appreciate what they see. Businesses can carry the same perspective. When a consumer sees your store, your website, your business card, your products, etc., you are hoping they see YOU.

Logos

Logos are a great way to establish visual representation of who you are in your business. By using graphic design, stylish fonts and artistic expression, logos serve as the face of your business, capturing consumer attention. When someone sees your logo, you want them to instantly remember you and your business that serves them.

Logos can only be beneficial if done strategically. They should answer the following questions when being developed:

Let There Be "A Brand"

- *What audience or demographic am I serving? What do they like?*
- *How will the logo relate to the products or services I sell?*
- *Will consumers understand the logo? Will it require explanation?*
- *Will the color(s) have significance?*
- *Will font type and size (or lack of font altogether) distract consumers away from the products and services?*
- *How will my logo differ from those in the same area of business?*

Missions and slogans

While visual identity is key for branding, having strong statements that are easy to remember and understand is also. Some consumers are not driven by visualization, but rather, by what the company stands for and upholds. Mental identity captures the mindset of consumers through both mission statements and company slogans. Mission statements define why a company exists, or states its purpose. Slogans can be short mottos that often describe the attitude behind the services and products that a business carries. The blend of a strong logo with powerful statements of purpose can attract consumers who feel connected to your brand. They feel that your business applies to their everyday lives.

Let There Be Business

Self-perception

Branding is not only visual and mental, but by now, you can see how branding can affect someone emotionally. Look at businesses around you. It is the athletic clothing that makes a young teen feel like he/she can be the best player on the field or court. It is the suit from a tailor with a slogan "Come in need, leave in demand" that can boost someone's self-perception and self-esteem. If your business can appeal to someone in an emotional way, they will always support, because you have impacted their personal growth.

Overall, branding adds legitimacy to a business. It lets the public know that not only is business identity important, but also how that identity related and influences potential consumers. You may not remember the CEO or founder of some businesses currently, but when you see a logo, read or hear a slogan or mission statement, your emotions reflect their impact. Branding can set you apart from competition and give paths for your vision to flourish. Confidence is key, also, because logos and slogans may not resonate immediately. But, if people can see your drive within your branding, they may remember and inquire more about you.

| 4 |

Let There BE "A Plan"

Writing The Plan For Your Business

"All you need is the plan, the road map, and the courage to press on to your destination"
- Earl Nightingale

Let There Be Business

It has been said those who fail to plan, plan to fail. Developing a business plan is very important when ensuring that you're on the right track with your business. The plan also serves as a guide towards helping to secure funding and finding out what you actually need for the business. Moreover, it helps you put your future commitments and thoughts to paper.

A business plan is used to identify those potential scenarios that you could face in starting your business. It also helps you set objectives by revealing those resources that may be required to achieve those goals. Business plans also help in ensuring that investors understand the scope of your business. It is a detailed method used to convey messages that most people aren't prepared to voice. However, in reading the plan, you can identify a method of communication that opens various barriers. Essentially, the business plan serves as a great resource of support. It provides an outlet for others to understand exactly how passionate you are about your business.

A well written business plan allows you to think outside of the box. It also allows you to become unemotional in your thinking, yet emotionally attached to the idea of starting your business. It helps to answer questions and assumptions while making planning much more affective. The business plan helps you to ensure the methods of integration as you are beginning your business and how you plan to operate your business.

Let There Be "A Plan"

Without a well-written business plan, clarification on how you see your business unfolding will be extremely hard. Establishing projections for the future, as well as determining if this is a financially profitable business (or if this is something you perhaps may want to turn into a nonprofit) will also be difficult. Security in writing a business plan for your business enables you to have direction and enables you to stay on course in your purpose.

What you will need to effectively write your business plan:

- *__Executive Summary__. This section provides a snippet of your business while introducing your business and operational goals.*
- *__Company Description__. This section provides information on what your business will do as well as how the company will achieve the goals.*
- *__Market Analysis__. This section examines your target audience, competitors and the location of your business.*
- *__Organization & Management__. This section provides information pertaining to the owner, employees and the style of business. This section will also discuss and identify your management style of how the business will function.*
- *__Services or products__. This section will identify the items sold within the business or the services you intend to provide.*

Let There Be Business

- **_Marketing and Sales_**. _This_ section will discuss your intentions to retrieve customers or clients. In addition, this section will discuss your business's marketing plan on profitability, productivity, and sustainability.

- **_Funding Request_**. _This_ section will highlight the finances you have obtained for start-up as well as the finances you are soliciting from various resources. This section should include the amount requesting as the business grows in the future.

- **_Financial Projections_**. _This_ section will discuss (in detail) every dollar contributed to the business. It will include historical data, prospective financial data. Historical data includes operating costs, cash flow, balance sheets and bank statements. Prospective financial data includes forecast of the business revenue in the future as well as quarterly and yearly projections.

- **_Appendix_**. _This_ section is not necessary. However, it is important to place your tables, graphs, photographs and detailed documents here as many lenders prefer to have visual support in addition to the written plan.

If you do not feel comfortable devising a business plan, it is okay. There are several companies and professionals that create business plans daily. These aspects are your basis for beginning.

| 5 |

Let There BE "Financing"
Securing Funding For Your Business

"Financing is tough, and you really have to work hard in the businesses you invest in"
-Greg Brenneman

Let There Be Business

Financing is a necessary aspect of any successful business. You may often hear business owners state "I am not in business for the money." However, without the money, you are not in business. This should not be taken as an insult to any potential consumer, for their support financially, mentally and emotionally is important to any business. If we are honest, we must understand that businesses seek to earn a profit. Otherwise, they could only exist as nonprofit organizations. When discussing finances, one must be mindful of how to secure proper funding as well as maintaining funds for future growth. In doing these things, businesses must show compassion to consumers and the communities from which they come.

Obtaining Funds

Let's say you want to buy a new car. You see one with the capability and amenities you want. That car costs $20,000. You don't have that amount in your personal savings. You have $5,000. What are your options? What should you do? Entrepreneurs face similar scenarios when trying to figure out the financial side to building a business. If funding isn't understood and obtained properly, the entrepreneur could overpay for things like equipment and staff, and could even fail and go bankrupt.

Back to the car example: the $5,000 in your personal savings could act as *seed money*. Although it may not be enough to complete the task at hand—in this case, buying the car, it can still serve as a catalyst to obtaining the rest.

So often, people underestimate the value of having great credit. Credit history allows individuals to show lenders that they are able to repay any amount borrowed. Job income, job history, personal expenses, major purchases, etc. help creditors decide if lending you money is beneficial or a mistake. Look at the $20,000 car as a $20,000 building that can potentially house a business.

Since $5,000 is clearly not enough, you may be thinking: "Well, just borrow another $15,000." While that sounds like accurate math, it isn't the best move necessarily. Instead of borrowing the 15K, you can strive to borrow more ($20-25K) to cover building costs, licensing, service equipment, etc., while using your $5,000 of personal money to create a savings, or nest egg for future purchases or emergencies. In the car example, this could mean maintenance, gas, or even car insurance. The amount of money loaned to you is based on your credit history and will have interest rates assigned by the banking or crediting institution. Still, there is yet another option.

You can attract investors by presenting a proposal of your business idea to individuals who support your dream. Sometimes, they like your idea and really want you to do well, so they will sow their own seed into your goal. Sometimes, they want nothing in return. There are instances where investors want to know how this product or service will benefit them, and may want to be involved in building it since their money is tied up in it. Either way, investing and loans are legitimate ways to obtain funding for a business idea. Be thorough in your planning, and your research. Like the car you hope to drive, you desire to build a business that will provide enough money to repay any loans you may have acquired as well as establish revenue for future business moves.

Maintaining Funds

Okay, so your business is starting and you are doing well. What will keep you making money? What will prevent you from going bankrupt and closing? Just as a new car will begin to age, so will your business. Cars need to be maintained to include oil changes, new brakes, new battery, and so much more. Unless you planned for these occurrences, they will always be an inconvenience. In the business realm, proper bookkeeping can help prevent the disappointment of facing unwanted costs. As profits come, one must set aside something for those unexpected (as well as expected) costs. If you know that licenses are to be renewed every year, then prepare for that.

Knowledge of taxation for the business can help keep an entrepreneur afloat year after year, and can create leeway to re-invest profits to improve the look, the products, and the location of the business. It is all about

Let There Be "Financing"

balance. You cannot save it all, nor should you spend it all. Invite experienced accountants and lawyers into your business structure when needed to make sure your finances remain intact.

Lastly, find a way to serve the community from which your consumers derive. If consumers feel that you are grateful for their support, and don't just view them as dollar signs, their support for you and your business will continue. Find a cause with which your business can help, and be genuine in your support. You will gain the love of those around you. Perhaps, when you need funds for something major (or unexpected like repairs from a severe storm), the community you serve will return service to you. Some things in life are bigger than money, even when you primarily are in business to make money.

| 6 |

Let There BE "A Location"
Planting Your Business In The Right Place

**"I'm easy. Put me in an interesting location
with good people and I'm there".
-Jane Curtin**

Let There Be Business

When establishing a new business, location is key and is essentially one of the most important in building a successful business. You must consider the style of business you are trying to attract. Examine the notions of wanting your business to be simple and chic or formal. You must decide if you want to be casual or if you want your location to be a place where people come and relax. Your location is a reflection of your image and the style of business you are intending to portray.

Aside from choosing a location, based off of operational measures or accessibility, it is also essential to choose a location based off of your target audience. Consider who your customers will be and how important the range from those customers to your business will be. Examine the community or area where your business will be located closely in an effort to ensure that your target audience matches the style of business you intend to grow.

Perhaps, you will need to complete a marketing analysis to obtain information on what that particular area or a location desires to see in business. It will also aid in identifying what resources would be there to help serve the population that is going to be supporting your business. Location also helps you determine price ranges.

There are certain things you should consider when choosing your location. For example, consider the your business needs, the employees, the equipment, the services, and most importantly consider the customers or clients. It is also important to examine your operations cost as far as the equipment that you need. Businesses should have adequate space to housed their equipment and products needed to enhance their services. For example, if you were in the business of being a distributor or selling T-shirts in bulk you would require an ample amount of space in order to secure your equipment as well as your inventory. It is definitely important to consider what your company has to offer as it relates to business services or products. When choosing your location, you also want to consider the convenience of your customers. When you center your business around location you can make it more convenient for customers to reach you.

Your location must be accessible to the audience you are trying to attract. The customers must feel safe when visiting your location. It is also important to consider parking. Most businesses fail because clients or customers feel there is not ample parking for them to get to the services. Most customers choose competitors due to convenience and something as simple as parking can be considered inconvenient and could also hurt your business. Most businesses, such as clothing stores are affected greatly by location. Customers may consider every component of your business when deciding to support. Several facets such as marketing, website branding, and social media have to target your audience. In order to increase your revenue or sales, your services must be number one – to include customer service in order to ensure duplication of clients. Lastly, consider your inventory. Nothing hurts a business worse than running out of those items that customers desire to have. Determine how much inventory you will need in order to identify the space that you need.

We are almost there. You have accomplished everything you need to begin your life as an entrepreneur. There is only one step left. It is now time to protect your investment.

| 7 |

Let There BE "Protection"
Developing Legal Structure In Your Business

"I'm Trusting in the Lord and a good lawyer"
-Oliver North

Let There Be Business

Studies show that upon developing or implementing a business, there are two important representatives that each entrepreneur should have - an accountant and lawyer. Ensuring that an attorney is always on retainer is very significant. Most attorneys provide assistance in almost every component of the business from compliance, copyrights and trademarks, and also in formulating business corporations. Most businesses feel as though an attorney is not needed until they have been summoned to court. However, having an attorney present in your business can ensure that you are not sued for services rendered or for misunderstandings between customer - client relations.

Essentially, attorneys also aid in reducing the amount of cost due to unresolved problems. Whether you're a large or small business, having an attorney present is highly advised. There are several types of attorneys. Most attorneys, as it pertains to business, are more skillful in the area of contracts, business organizations, real estate, (as it pertains to your location) taxes, and licenses (as it ensures that you're in compliance with both federal and state taxes). They also specialize in ensuring that while you're promoting your business that all of your property is in interest or that your brand or trademark copyright carries protections to assist in keeping others from duplicating your business.

Let There Be "Protection"

There are several questions you should ask upon selecting an attorney for your business. You should always ensure that your attorney has experience. Never be afraid to ask direct questions as it pertains to your attorney's experience, for most attorneys are not familiar with every area of law. Be sure to ask if they are familiar with business practices such as business law, copyright laws, trademark infringement laws, duplication of services and products. You may also want to ensure that your attorney has experience in representing others in a similar interest or business as it could eventually be a conflict if your attorney is not experienced or well versed. Always ensure there is always a good legal code of ethics when selecting your attorney and be very receptive and open minded to the advice given by your legal team.

Often times, business owners neglect the responsibility of retaining attorney as they feel as though they are very expensive. However, there are numerous amounts of affiliated groups and attorneys that work in the concept of small business. If in doubt, refer to your local attorney listing. You also have the opportunity of securing an attorney by looking at the American Bar Association. This website will provide information about professionals who have legal answers.

| Conclusion |

Let There Be Business is an inspirational, yet educational book designed to help and motivate business owners into speaking directly to their businesses. It serves as a guide, composed of 7 key components. *Let There Be Business* is an opportunity for people to understand how much power we have into speaking success into our own lives. It does not take away from the roles of mentors, leaders, and/or authoritative figures that have the power to enhance what is already established.

This book will propel your mind into thinking what can be done and how it can be done. Reading this should enable you to effectively plan the rest of your business life. You may take away certain ideas that not only apply professionally, but also personally. *Let There Be Business* was designed to speak directly to you. So, I want you to remain focused, driven, and passionate about your dreams. Even when you feel as though you will not fulfill them, or even if you need to alter your steps, be encouraged and don't give up!

| Resources |

Chapter 1   **Let There BE "An Idea"**
Making It All Make Sense

Adams, Susan. (2013). *4 Steps To Successful Brainstorming.*
    Retrieved June 2, 2017 from www.forbes.com

Firestone, Harvey. (2017). *Why Brainstorming Is A Crucial
    Element in Business. Retrieved May 14, 2017 from
    www.aib.edu.au*

_____

Chapter 2   **Let There BE "Training & Education"**
Seeking Counsel Prior To Beginning Business

Frost, Shelley. (2016). *The Importance of Training &
    Development In The Workplace. Retrieved May 14,
    2017 from www.smallbusiness.chron.com*

Education and Training Business & Franchise Opportunities.
    (2017). Retrieved from www.entrepreneur.com

_____

Chapter 3   **Let There BE "A Brand"**
Securing The Identity Of Your Business
Separating Professional From Personal

The Basics of Branding. (2017). Retrieved June 2, 2017
from www.entreprenuer.com

———————

Chapter 4   Let There BE "A Plan"
Writing The Plan For Your Business

Millyard, Kath. (2017). What Is the Importance & Purpose of
a Business Plan? Retrieved June 2, 2017 from
www.smallbusiness.chron.com

———————

Chapter 5   Let There BE "Financing"
Securing Funding For Your Business

Duff, Victoria. (2016). Importance of Finance & Its Role
Within Business. Retrieved May 13, 2017 from
www.smallbusiness.chron.com

Griffin, Dana. (2016). Role of Finance in a Business. Retrieved
May, 13, 2017 from www.smallbusiness.chron.com

———————

Chapter 6   Let There BE "A Location"
Planting Your Business in the Right Place

Choose a Location. (2016). Retrieved May 13, 2017 from
www.businessgov.au

Chapter 7   Let There BE "Protection"
Developing Legal Structure In Your Business

Onibalusi, Ayodeji. (2016). *5 Ways to Protect Your Small Business Against Legal Fallout. Retrieved June 30, 2017 from* www.entrepreneur.com

———————————

Additional Resources

www.legalshield.com

www.ebonyivoryps.com

www.sba.gov

www.nfib.com

www.score.org

www.usa.gov

www.nbea.org

| Acknowledgements |

I wish to thank all of the wonderful people who served as fuel to my spirit while on my journey to be what I define as "Great". I would like to thank God for trusting me with the gift to serve others. I did not see your plan for my life or the route I would take to get here but I thank you for being here with me every step of the way. This is for you and for your glory. To my deceased father, the late Tyrone Acker, long after your death, the magic from your presence still exists. There will never be another you but I will indeed carry your name and legacy proudly to create, if only in words and paper, the dreams and visions you had for my life. To my mother, Alice Acker, you are a natural warrior. My hidden strength flows from you. The courage you had to defend yourself, while defending this country is why I walk proudly knowing the life I missed out on with you was one that you protected, and still protect to this day. Thank you for making me the woman that I am.... strong and determined. To my children, Trey and Trinity, thank you for making me your mother. I am so proud and humble that God chose me for the both of you. I love you both beyond the word. To the world's best girl pals.... Thank you is meaningless when it comes to the sacrifices you have made just being my friends. Shennel, thank you for your educational insight and wisdom. Nicole, thank you for your meekness and endless smile. Earikka, you understand me when I don't understand myself. Thank you for always seeing the "bright side". MarQuiesha, thank you for crying with me, smiling with me, and always making me feel like it was going to be ok even if you didn't believe it would be. Joye, thank for wearing the title of "best friend" when I could not always fulfill the role. Michole, thank you for being the "cost conscious" friend. Thank you for showing the way when there was no way. Tiffani, thank you for praying without cease. The constant motivation was always appreciated. Sheila, your smile is contagious. Although you don't say much, I always feel your presence. Katherine, thank you for your push and your ability to make me look beautiful in every photo. I love your genuine spirit. Kasie and Atowanna, you both know just what to say and when to say that. Despite the distance, you are always close. Tonya, whenever there is a need to uplift, there you are. Thank you so much. Chasity, thank you for pushing and promoting EIPS to endless measures. I truly appreciate it. To my family, thank you is not enough. I value and appreciate each of you. Thank you Avery for being my mentor and for being the best at everything you do. Thank you Erica and the girls for sharing him with me. To Teara, thank you for always giving me light in my darkest times. I am proud and I am forever grateful. To John and Angela, you two are the epitome of family.... Thank you. Minktoy, there is not enough room on this page to describe how much grace, humility and love I have developed for you. You will always have a seat at every table I'm invited to. Angela & Amira, thank you for taking care of my most prize processions as I journeyed to be great. To one of my favorite teachers, Judy Whilhite- Mincey, thank you for teaching me my most valuable asset. Without you, this may not have been possible. To my spiritual leaders, (both past and present) Dr. Eric D. Mason, Sr. and Pastor Damion P. Gordon, thank you. Everything that you have taught me has not fallen on deaf ears. I have been listening and I hope that I am representing you both to the highest level of servanthood and Christianity possible. Pastor Gordon, "Keep Digging"... You are almost done. To my business colleagues and supporters.... Thank you. Last but not least, to the man that has stolen my heart for all the right reasons... thank you. My professionalism, my brand, my business savvy, the wisdom, the insight, the hindsight, the late night brainstorms, the growth, the exposure, the risks and the rewards are all because of you. You pushed me further than I have ever been pushed. Thank you for seeing me for whom I was and not wanting to change a thing. I love you so much Kenneth Brown. You spoke the words to me over a year ago and now it's a book. I took your lead and I said LET THERE BE...

Martin Jonque – Thank you for pushing the envelope on this project. For listening to the realms of business versus that of people. I humbly thank you and appreciate every effort made for me and EIPS.

Dr. Casteel & Mr. Moses Calhoun – Thank you for being my friends, business mentors and most of all "My Frats"

Stacie Coppock, Melanie Jo, James Oliver, Lorenzo McDonald and Monica Daughtry – Thank You for being the first to support me on every social media post, every workshop or conference and increasing the name of EIPS, INC. in various households. It did not go unnoticed.... In fact, it helped me #GETNOTICED!

Let There Be...

-T.A.